BE A CONSTRUCTION EQUIPMENT OPERATOR

GUIDE TO THE TRADES

Published in the United States of America by Cherry Lake Publishing
Ann Arbor, Michigan
www.cherrylakepublishing.com

Reading Adviser: Marla Conn, MS, Ed., Literacy specialist, Read-Ability, Inc.

Photo Credits: Cover and page 1, ©Linus Strandholm/Shutterstock; page 5, ©GIRODJL/Shutterstock; pages 6 and 22, ©michaeljung/Shutterstock; page 8, ©Oleg Totskyi/Shutterstock; page 11, ©SpeedKingz/Shutterstock; page 12, ©Monkey Business Images/Shutterstock; page 14, ©sima/Shutterstock; page 16, ©Mikbiz/Shutterstock; page 19, ©sirtravelot/Shutterstock; page 20, ©Roman023_photography/Shutterstock; page 25, ©Stockr/Shutterstock; page 26, ©inacio pires/Shutterstock; page 28, ©Wollertz/Shutterstock

Library of Congress Cataloging-in-Publication Data
Names: Mara, Wil, author.
Title: Be a construction equipment operator / by Wil Mara.
Description: Ann Arbor, Michigan : Cherry Lake Publishing, [2019] | Series: 21st century skills library | Includes bibliographical references and index.
Identifiers: LCCN 2019003501| ISBN 9781534148215 (lib. bdg.) | ISBN 9781534149649 (pdf) | ISBN 9781534151079 (pbk.) | ISBN 9781534152502 (ebook)
Subjects: LCSH: Building—Vocational guidance—Juvenile literature. | Construction industry—Vocational guidance—Juvenile literature. | Construction equipment—Juvenile literature. | Construction equipment operators—Juvenile literature.
Classification: LCC TH159 .M37 2019 | DDC 690.028/4—dc23
LC record available at https://lccn.loc.gov/2019003501

Cherry Lake Publishing would like to acknowledge the work of The Partnership for 21st Century Learning. Please visit *www.p21.org* for more information.

Printed in the United States of America
Corporate Graphics

ABOUT THE AUTHOR

Wil Mara is the author of over 175 fiction and nonfiction books for children. He has written many titles for Cherry Lake Publishing, including the popular *Global Citizens: Modern Media* and *Citizen's Guide* series. More about his work can be found at www.wilmara.com.

TABLE OF CONTENTS

CHAPTER 1

Very Heavy Equipment

Katie Milligan wakes up before the sun rises. She stretches her arms and yawns to start the new day. After showering and dressing, she heads outside to her pickup truck. She makes a quick stop at a local café for a cup of coffee and a doughnut, and then she's on her way to work.

Katie doesn't have an office. She doesn't sit behind a desk or work at a computer. In fact, her workplace changes all the time. Every day, she goes to a job **site**. Most of the time, the site is a place where a new home or building is being constructed. Katie has done a lot of construction jobs over the years. She has helped build everything from stores and

A construction equipment operator can use a backhoe to dig massive holes very quickly.

restaurants to hospitals and schools. She's a construction equipment operator, which means she works the big vehicles and other machines that make construction possible. She drives **pavers** to create perfectly flat parking lots. She uses **backhoes** to dig huge holes at the start of construction projects. Cranes make it possible for her to lift enormous pieces of metal high into the air. And these are just some of the incredible machines that can be found at construction sites.

A foreman works closely with equipment operators and other workers on a construction site to make sure each job goes smoothly.

Katie arrives at the day's job site at about 7:30 a.m. Many other workers are already there. The first thing Katie does is visit the **foreman**. The foreman oversees the entire operation. He tells Katie what needs to be done each day. They review some **blueprints** together. On this job, they're constructing a strip mall. They've been working on it for three months now, and they've got at least another two to go. Katie really enjoys the fact that each job is a little different from the last. She's even done some **demolition** work, which requires heavy equipment as part of the cleanup process. Each new job presents unique challenges, and Katie always learns a few things she didn't know before.

Today, tons of sand and gravel have to be moved from one area of the site to another. Right now, this material is sitting in giant piles near the road. But it needs to be packed around the **foundation** of the strip mall to strengthen it. Katie gets into a front-end **loader** to do the job. This is a tractor-like vehicle with an enormous bucket at the front. The bucket can be used to scoop and carry just about anything.

21st Century Content

There are about 430,000 construction equipment operators working in the United States. The states that employ the most operators are listed here:

- Texas—38,500
- California—26,000
- Pennsylvania—20,500
- Florida—16,000
- Ohio—16,000

Crane operators sometimes sit high above the ground.

Katie starts up the loader and gets moving. She scoops up the sand and gravel one bucketful at a time. She knows exactly how much she can safely carry at a time. Once the bucket is full, she drives over to the edge of the foundation and dumps it into the hole. It is slow-going work, but she doesn't mind.

Katie loves working the front-end loader. She has been a construction equipment operator for more than 20 years now. But she never gets tired of the feeling of driving these powerful machines. Just by working the controls, she can move more material in a day than a whole team of people could in a week using shovels and wheelbarrows.

Katie also loves working outside. This is a good thing, because her job takes place almost entirely outdoors. On some days, the weather turns nasty. But even wind, rain, and snow don't bother Katie. She's usually inside the **cab** of her vehicle. Most cabs are fully enclosed and even have heating and air-conditioning systems.

Katie takes one break during the day for lunch. This is when she hangs out with the other workers. She's friends with many of them, and she likes the social part of her job. It's the best of both worlds. She gets to talk with the others for a while, and then she goes back to the front-end loader and works by herself. It's a perfect balance.

The workday ends around 5:00 p.m. By then, Katie is usually pretty tired. Even though the machinery does most of the heavy lifting, operating it all day long is hard work. It's all worth it, though. Once that strip mall is ready for business, Katie's going to do a little shopping there with her family. While she's there, she'll be able to think to herself, *I helped build this.*

CHAPTER 2

Becoming an Operator

Studying to become a construction equipment operator may not require a college degree, but it still takes a lot of hard work. Training in this field requires focused, specialized education. Students must accumulate a great deal of hands-on experience before they are able to start working as professionals. After all, heavy construction equipment can be very dangerous if used incorrectly. It takes a lot of knowledge and skill to operate this machinery the right way.

The first step on the path to becoming a construction equipment operator is high school. Students won't get the opportunity to drive bulldozers or backhoes during this time. However, there is still plenty for them to learn. Math skills will

Anyone who is thinking of becoming an equipment operator should pay close attention to science and math classes in school.

be extremely important throughout an operator's entire career. Studying hard in high school math classes will ensure that future operators are able to perform the calculations that are a daily part of their job. For example, equipment operators must be able to determine how much something weighs before picking it up with a machine. Such measurements need to be fairly precise. Simple guesswork will not do.

Another class to pay particular attention to in high school is physics. Knowledge of this branch of science will help

Learning how to work on cars is a good introduction to making repairs on bigger machines.

operators determine the correct way to lift and move objects of different sizes, shapes, and weights.

Automotive classes are also very useful for future equipment operators. Part of an operator's job involves caring for their equipment and making minor repairs as needed. This requires a good knowledge of how engines and other machine parts work.

After graduating from high school, aspiring construction equipment operators often enroll in some kind of secondary school. This could be a trade or vocational school. It could also be a two-year college offering an associate's degree. At any of these schools, students can begin training to use a variety of construction equipment.

During their time in secondary school, future operators study job-specific mathematics and learn about different kinds of heavy equipment. They learn how to operate different machines safely and complete different kinds of jobs. Students don't just read about these things in classrooms. They also get plenty of firsthand experience. Under the supervision of their

Some construction equipment can be driven around much like a car. Each machine has different controls that the operator must learn.

teachers, they practice operating loaders, dump trucks, tractors, and other equipment. They haul heavy loads from one place to another and guide heavy beams onto structures. This hands-on experience ensures that they will be prepared to start working on real job sites as soon as they graduate.

After completing a trade or vocational program, student operators likely have a pretty good understanding of construction equipment. However, they are not quite ready to start working on their own. Instead, they must spend some time as **apprentices**. During an apprenticeship, a young operator works under the careful supervision of a much more experienced **mentor**. They complete real work on real job sites. The mentor observes and offers guidance or assistance

Life and Career Skills

Certain types of construction equipment require advanced training and certification. For example, the use of most cranes requires approval from the National Commission for the Certification of Crane Operators (NCCCO). Procedures for obtaining a crane **license** vary by state. However, an applicant usually needs to take a physical exam, pass a written test, and demonstrate safe crane operation.

Crane operators earn an average annual wage of around $52,000. Employment of crane and tower operators is expected to increase more quickly than most other professions. Much of this growth will result from increases in global shipping, which will require more professionals to help with loading and unloading.

Being able to drive equipment on regular roads enables operators to transport heavy loads from one site to another.

when needed. Over the course of the apprenticeship, the mentor and the apprentice often form a close bond.

The length of apprenticeship programs varies from state to state. However, the average time is between three and four years. Generally speaking, apprenticeship programs are sponsored either through the state or through an operators' **union**. Not everyone who applies for a construction equipment operator apprenticeship is accepted. Students who got good grades in school are most likely to be chosen as apprentices.

Following an apprenticeship, an operator has to earn a license before being allowed to finally work independently. The requirements for becoming licensed vary from state to state. They usually require a certain amount of experience. Some states have separate licenses for different types of construction equipment. For example, an operator might need one license to operate a bulldozer and a different one for a backhoe.

In many places, a construction equipment operator is also expected to have a commercial driver's license. This is a special type of driver's license that allows holders to drive large vehicles such as dump trucks and semi trucks on public roads. Having one of these is important to equipment operators. It enables them to transport loads not just within a job site but also from one site to another.

In many states, a license to operate construction machinery is not issued for life. The operator may have to re-qualify for it every so often. This ensures that the operator's skills and knowledge are up-to-date.

CHAPTER 3

On the Job

A career as a construction equipment operator can be very satisfying and rewarding. It is also a unique line of work that stands out from other jobs in the building trades. And if you have the right personality and skills, it could be the perfect profession for you.

Perhaps above all else, an operator needs to have natural mechanical abilities. Some people seem to have a built-in curiosity about machines. They are able to figure out pretty easily how different machines work. They are the sort of people who like to take things apart to see how they work. As kids, they probably liked to build things and play with toy

Operating construction equipment requires intense focus. Operators should be able to notice small details that could be warning signs of trouble ahead.

When moving heavy objects such as concrete beams into position, an operator cannot afford to make mistakes.

vehicles. These people are often perfect candidates to become construction equipment operators.

Picture an operator who is lowering massive concrete pipes into the ground to install a sewer line. They need to have a feel for when the loader they're driving is too stressed by the weight. If they've been using the vehicle for many weeks, they need to know when it needs maintenance. Formal education can help in this area. But many construction equipment operators also rely on a natural sense of whether or not their machines are working. They "become one" with their machines and can sense things that others might not. Someone who lacks a natural interest in mechanical devices likely won't understand this.

A good construction equipment operator is also the type of person who enjoys paying attention to detail. In a job where safety is critical and serious accidents are always possible, operators constantly need to be on high alert. They must take the time to check over all equipment before the work begins. They carefully evaluate loads, test soil compaction caused by the weight of their machines, and much more. Every detail is important. Operators would rather leave as little to chance as possible. They know how to seek out the most important details and how to evaluate them as a whole to see the bigger picture.

The best construction equipment operators are also good at dealing with people. Even though operators often work by themselves, they still need to coordinate with others on a regular basis. Every construction site requires a team, and a team has to work together to be effective. Sometimes this

When in the cab of a machine, an operator can use a radio to stay in touch with the foreman or other workers on the site.

means working together and coming up with ideas to solve problems. Other times, it means knowing when to simply do as someone else instructs.

An operator should be the kind of person who can solve a problem on the spot. Not all projects will go smoothly. Deliveries can be late, workers can get sick, and equipment can break down. These situations can be stressful when working on a deadline. A good equipment operator is able to remain calm and think clearly when getting bad news. Instead of getting angry or worried, an operator determines the exact problem, analyzes its cause, then creates a fast but effective plan to fix it.

21st Century Content

Construction equipment operators can choose to work in several different industries. Each carries its own risks and rewards, and some pay a little better than others. Here are some of the most common industries that employ equipment operators, along with the average salaries they pay:

- Building construction—$53,180
- Civil engineering—$49,440
- Specialty trade contracting—$45,530
- Mining and quarrying, including oil and gas extraction—$45,380
- Local government construction—$41,370

CHAPTER 4

Rules and Regulations

Heavy construction equipment is both expensive and dangerous. Operating these machines is a big responsibility. Mistakes can damage buildings or equipment and cost a lot of money. They could also cause serious injuries. As a result, there are many laws and regulations in place to ensure that such accidents do not happen often. Regulations also protect operators from legal troubles and keep them safe on the job.

Anyone involved in the building trades needs to have a strong understanding of local construction **codes**. These are sets of guidelines that determine exactly how a building can and can't be put together. For example, during the

Asphalt rollers are used to smooth out roads, parking lots, and other flat surfaces.

construction of an office building, there will be a series of beams within the structure that are designed to hold a great amount of weight. These are often referred to as load-bearing structures. A construction equipment operator might be responsible for setting these in place. If they aren't strong enough or have been cut to improper lengths, there will be a weakness in the building. At some point in the future, they could give way. This could cause parts of the building to

A bulldozer is an expensive, complex piece of machinery.

collapse. Construction codes are put in place to avoid these kinds of problems. Construction equipment operators should know the codes and call attention to any violations they notice while on a job site.

Life and Career Skills

Some operators reach a point in their career where they wish to purchase their own construction equipment. For example, they might want to open their own business instead of working for someone else. Operators who take this step need to purchase insurance for their equipment.

Construction vehicles and other heavy machinery can experience problems beyond mechanical malfunction. Bad weather can cause damage to equipment that is left outside. This happens somewhat often, since it is usually impractical to bring heavy equipment inside at the end of each workday. Equipment can also become the target of vandalism or theft. Vandals can easily render a loader or dozer inoperable. Thieves are drawn to such equipment because of the high price tags involved. A new bulldozer, for example, can cost anywhere from $30,000 to $200,000! As long as operators have taken out good insurance policies, they don't have to worry about these issues. Their insurance will cover the costs.

Operators usually have to climb ladders to reach the cabs of their machines.

Similarly, construction equipment operators should be aware of local safety requirements. There is a branch of the United States Department of Labor known as the Occupational Safety and Health Administration (OSHA). The purpose of OSHA is to provide safe working conditions for all people. This is particularly important at construction sites, where the chances of injury are greater than in many other jobs. Construction equipment operators should always be aware of the working conditions around them. They should keep a look out for potentially dangerous materials or poorly maintained equipment. OSHA has the right to inspect work sites whenever it wishes. It can shut down a project entirely if it determines that a site doesn't meet safety standards. Good construction equipment operators report safety concerns to their managers. This not only helps avoid problems with OSHA but also minimizes the risk of injury to themselves or others.

Luckily, these kinds of issues are not usually a problem for most operators. While they always keep an eye on safety, they usually get to spend most of the time doing what they do best: getting behind the controls of incredible machines and building things!

Think About It

Humans have been finding new ways to build great structures for thousands of years. The ancient Romans created simple cranes from pulleys and ropes. Early forms of heavy machinery were powered by the efforts of humans or large animals. This did not change until the 1800s, when steam engines became common. What kinds of problems do you suppose the earliest builders encountered? What were the greatest dangers they faced? How do you think they overcame these issues? What made them work so hard to create new and improved methods of construction?

Construction equipment operators work with many different machines and vehicles over the course of their careers. Which machines are most interesting to you? Explain your answer in as much detail as possible. What parts of the job do you think you'd enjoy the most? Why?

Find Out More

BOOKS

Capici, Gaetano. *What Does It Do? Cement Mixer.* Ann Arbor, MI: Cherry Lake Publishing, 2011.

Rhatigan, Joe. *Get a Job at the Construction Site.* Ann Arbor, MI: Cherry Lake Publishing, 2017.

Zeiger, Jennifer. *What Does It Do? Dump Truck.* Ann Arbor, MI: Cherry Lake Publishing, 2011.

WEBSITES

PBS—Building Big
www.pbs.org/wgbh/buildingbig
Find out what it takes to construct large structures such as bridges, dams, and skyscrapers.

U.S. Bureau of Labor Statistics—Occupational Outlook Handbook: Construction Equipment Operators
https://www.bls.gov/ooh/construction-and-extraction/construction-equipment-operators.htm
Learn how to become an equipment operator and find out more about the profession at this government site.

GLOSSARY

apprentices (uh-PREN-tis-iz) people who are learning a skill by working with an expert on the job

backhoes (BAK-hohz) construction vehicles designed to dig large holes

blueprints (BLOO-printz) drawings that illustrate how a structure needs to be built

cab (KAB) the enclosed part of a heavy construction vehicle where the operator sits and works the controls

codes (KOHDZ) rules that determine the correct design and construction of buildings

demolition (dem-uh-LISH-uhn) the process of destroying part or all of an existing structure

foreman (FOR-muhn) the person in charge of a construction job

foundation (foun-DAY-shuhn) the lowest level of a structure, upon which the rest of the structure is built

license (LYE-suhns) an official certification that someone is qualified to perform a job

loader (LOH-dur) a construction vehicle designed to lift and move large amounts of heavy material

mentor (MEN-tor) someone who teaches a less experienced person

pavers (PAY-vurz) construction vehicles designed to lay smooth paving on otherwise rough and unpaved surfaces, such as dirt or gravel

site (SITE) location of a construction job

union (YOON-yuhn) an organization that protects the interests of a certain type of worker, such as a construction equipment operator

INDEX